The Big Golden Book of
THE WILD WEST
American Indians, Cowboys,
and the Settling of the West

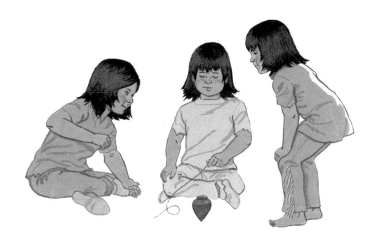

For my daughter and son,
Melissa and Barr,
and their great-great grandmother
Aimée Priestley Osbourne,
an American Pioneer

Text Consultant: Judith A. Brundin,
Supervisory Educational Specialist,
National Museum of the American Indian,
Smithsonian Institution, New York

The Big Golden Book of
THE WILD WEST
American Indians, Cowboys, and the Settling of the West

By Gina Ingoglia
Illustrated by Gene Biggs

A GOLDEN BOOK • NEW YORK
Western Publishing Company, Inc., Racine, Wisconsin 53404

A   MCMXCI

TABLE OF CONTENTS

Some games required not the luck of the dice, but great skill. The players shot arrows through wooden hoops with mesh centers. The holes in the mesh were worth different points. Mandan men and boys also held rapid-fire contests with arrows. They tried to see who could shoot the most arrows into the air before any fell to the ground. Some archers could keep eight arrows flying at once!

The Zuni stuck sharp sticks into the ends of dried corncobs to make darts. They attached turkey feathers to the cobs to help them fly toward the target.

Many Indians played a game called shinny, with a leather ball the size of a large grapefruit and a wooden stick that looked like a short, modern hockey stick. As many as 80 to 100 people played at a time. Sometimes men and women played shinny together. They could kick the ball or hit it with the stick, but they weren't allowed to touch it with their hands.

Each year tribes gathered for buffalo hunts. Before the hunts they often played team games. They ran relay races and raced on horseback. Everybody looked forward to these games of friendly rivalry and sportsmanship.

Sacagawea and the Lewis and Clark Expedition

In 1803 President Thomas Jefferson asked Meriwether Lewis and William Clark to plan a long trip called an expedition. The President wanted the two men to cross America to the Pacific Ocean, report what they saw, and set up fur-trading routes with the Indians.

The explorers trained a team of men for the hard western trip in North Dakota, near a Hidatsa village. A French fur trader named Toussaint Charbonneau (Too-SAHN SHAR-bon-no) and his 19-year-old Indian wife, Sacagawea (SACK-uh-ja-WE-uh), lived nearby. Sacagawea was a Shoshone (Show-show-nee) Indian who was born and raised in the area now called Montana and Idaho. When she was about 14 years old, Sacagawea was kidnapped by a band of attacking Hidatsas, who took her to their village.

Lewis and Clark hired Charbonneau to be their guide. They especially wanted Sacagawea to come. She spoke the Shoshone language and could translate for Lewis and Clark when the expedition traveled through her homeland. Even though she had a new baby son to care for, Sacagawea wanted to go and took the baby along on the trip. For the young Indian woman, joining the expedition meant seeing her family again.

The explorers carried valuable books and scientific instruments. One day during the long journey a canoe filled with water and much of the precious cargo floated into the river. Sacagawea was the one who acted quickly and rescued the equipment.

When they reached the Shoshone, the young woman talked with her brother, who was the Indians' chief. She arranged for the fresh horses the men needed to cross the Rocky Mountains.

The Lewis and Clark expedition covered almost 2,000 miles and lasted 18 months. The explorers wrote descriptions of the Indian tribes and the western landscape, including its animals and plants. When they returned, the men brought back two bear cubs for President Jefferson.

In his long reports describing the expedition, Meriwether Lewis often noted Sacagawea's bravery and great assistance. Without her help the Lewis and Clark expedition would not have been the great success that it was.

Some history books say Sacagawea died when she was only 25 years old. Others say she went home to the Shoshone and lived a long life. It will probably always be a mystery. Today there are many statues honoring Sacagawea in parks and cities throughout the United States.

An Artist Who "Captured" the West

Twenty-five years after the Lewis and Clark Expedition, an eager artist from Philadelphia, Pennsylvania, packed up his paints, canvases, and notebooks and headed west. His name was George Catlin.

He had heard stories about the Indian people and wanted to see what they were like. The mysterious West sounded like a wonderful place to paint. It proved to be very fortunate for us that he went. Those were the days before photographs, and this artistic explorer recorded western life that we otherwise would never have seen.

Between 1830 and 1836, George Catlin hiked miles and miles over lonely western plains. He produced more than 600 paintings in spite of hard conditions. The weather was often bad, and studying wild animals was dangerous. But nothing escaped this artist's eyes. Besides his handsome paintings, he took careful notes and made numerous sketches.

He got to know the Indians very well, visiting 48 tribes. Many of them had never seen a white man before, but they made George Catlin feel at home, and he became their friend.

The artist painted pictures of the Indians' daily lives. He wrote down what they wore, what they ate, and where they lived. He learned about their religious ceremonies, followed them on buffalo hunts, and watched the games they played. Some of his most important contributions to history were his fine portraits of Indian chiefs.

After George Catlin took his paintings back home, they toured cities in the United States and Europe for the next 30 years. Catlin's Indian Gallery, as his works were called, introduced many Americans and Europeans to the American West. Today these paintings hang in the Smithsonian Institution in Washington, D.C.

Wagon Trains

As more fascinating news of the West traveled back east, more and more people grew curious and decided to move there. Western fever was sweeping the country.

The first adventurous families set out for the open prairies (as the plains were also called) in 1841. Some of those heading west had already been pioneers in eastern wildernesses. They had cleared forested land, built log cabins, and started farms. But raising crops in rocky eastern soil wasn't always easy. The West sounded like a good place to start again. There would surely be lots of space!

The families that were moving had mixed feelings of excitement, sorrow, and fear. They looked forward to a more profitable life, but it was hard to leave loving relatives and friends. Stories of Indian attacks also worried them.

The pioneers traveled in canvas-covered wagons that were usually drawn by four oxen. The wagons were never big enough to hold every precious possession. Families took only what they wouldn't be able to make themselves. Cooking utensils, iron pots, and kettles were carefully packed. Necessary items like axes, hoes, plows, rifles, and molds for making bullets were never left behind. Sometimes the pioneers tucked in a few flowering plants to brighten their new homes and to remind them of the lands they were leaving. Each child was sure to add a favorite toy to the wagonload.

Pioneer families didn't cross the open prairie alone. They joined together for companionship and safety. Wagons gathered in towns called "jumping-off places" where long trails led west. The most popular jumping-off place was Independence, Missouri. The wagons lined up and formed long wagon trains. Then, together, everyone headed west—to unknown lands and new lives.

On the Trail

The flat prairie stretched ahead of the traveling pioneers like an endless grassy sea. For this reason their covered wagons were called prairie schooners (SKOO-ners)—named for schooner ships that sailed across the oceans.

Each wagon train elected a leader and hired a scout. Scouts knew where to find food and water. They also planned the distances the wagons had to travel each day. The pioneers had to be settled by spring planting time, or they wouldn't have food for winter.

It took months to make the difficult trip. There were dangerous tornadoes, blinding sandstorms, flash floods, and even quicksand. Tall grasses hid poisonous snakes and, at night, wolves howled close by. Sometimes buffalo herds stampeded through the wagon trains.

Although the travelers worried about Indian attacks, there were very few raids on wagon trains during this period. The Indians often traded meat and fish in exchange for glass beads and cloth that the travelers brought along especially to trade. This was very helpful to the pioneers, since most of them were farmers and not experienced hunters or fishermen.

Sometimes the Indians asked the pioneers for food. Many of the pioneers thought the Indians were begging, but they were wrong. The Indians believed that sharing food was a sign of peace and friendship. Because the settlers didn't understand the Indians' beliefs and customs, they often misjudged them.

Schooner rides were very bumpy! And wagons often broke down or became stuck in deep ruts along the trail. Sometimes the wagons had to cross wide rivers with dangerous currents. The pioneers often hired Indians, who were excellent swimmers, to lead their frightened animals through the rushing waters.

When a river was too deep for the wagons to cross, the travelers took the wagons apart. On rafts or in canoes, Indians ferried the pioneers, their supplies, and the wagon parts across the river. Once safe on the other side, the pioneers put their wagons back together and continued the journey west.

Dalton Gang

Jesse James

Western Villains

The growing West was known for its lawlessness. Outlaws robbed banks, held up trains, and stole jewels and money from people on stagecoaches. Criminals like the Dalton Gang, Jesse James, and Billy the Kid were known throughout the country. Most of them died in gunfights when they were still young.

Men were not the only people who broke the law. One of the West's most famous bandits and horse thieves was a woman named Belle Starr. Belle usually wore gold earrings, a large Mexican hat, and a velvet skirt. People told wild tales about Belle. Once, they said, she was being chased by a town sheriff and a group of his men, called a posse (poss-see). Supposedly Belle told the local blacksmith to remove her horse's shoes as fast as possible and nail them on backward. Then she rode off to escape

Billy the Kid

Black Bart

Belle Starr

the posse. When the posse found her horse's tracks, the men thought she'd ridden away in the other direction!

In 1889, Belle Starr was killed—shot in the back by a stranger.

Black Bart was a robber who had an original way of disguising himself. He made a mask out of an old flour sack and pulled it over his head when he began a robbery. Black Bart held up Wells Fargo stage-coaches for money kept on board in a box. This bandit never rode a horse. He jumped out from behind bushes, stopped the stagecoach, and demanded the box. Then he took out a little hatchet he carried with him and chopped open the box. He emptied out the money and put a handwritten poem inside the box.

Black Bart, the poet-thief, was finally caught and sent to prison.

Barbed Wire

In the early 1870's a farmer from Illinois named Joseph Glidden invented a new kind of fencing called barbed wire. Sharp metal "barbs" were attached to the new fence wire. This discouraged animals from attempting to climb it. Glidden's company was successful, and the operation was speedy. Workers could manufacture 600 miles of barbed wire in only 10 hours! During the 1880's barbed wire went up everywhere and helped change the West still further.

To keep neighboring cattle from grazing on their land, some ranchers put up many miles of barbed wire. However, the heaviest snows in history fell during the winter of 1885. Herds of frantic animals struggled to escape the deep drifts. The barbed wire fences trapped them, and the animals crushed each other to death. With their cattle dead, many ranchers went out of business.

Farmers, cattlemen, and sheepherders in the West often fought with each other. Farmers put up barbed wire to keep cattle and sheep from trampling their crops. Sheepherders put up barbed wire to keep cattle away from their flocks.

By the late 1800's train tracks crossed the entire country. Puffing steam engines pulled freight cars to all parts of the West. The trains also brought more settlers. Many Chinese workers and some Indians helped to build the railroads. But most of the Indian tribes were furious because their land was being scarred and taken over. They attacked railroad workers and passengers. On dark nights, when no one could see them, members of tribes often tore up the tracks.

The buffalo were almost gone. Professional hunters had killed most of them. People paid high prices in eastern cities for buffalo robes—warm blankets made from hides. People also thought buffalo tongue was a special treat to eat. Buffalo hunting was so popular that tourists shot grazing buffalo from train windows just to see how many they could hit.

For the first time, some Indians began to hunt more of their sacred buffalo than they needed. They sold the tongues and hides at the settlers' trading posts in exchange for guns and tools. Rotting bodies of dead buffalo were scattered all over the plains. It was a tragic time for the West.